CONTENTS

I0048256

FROM THE EDITOR

Welcome to the new year!

Shelby Jo Long is our featured author in this edition. Shelby is the senior vice president and co-owner of the Strategic Advisor Board. She is also a co-owner of Rogue Publishing Partners and the founder of The Genius Project.

Shelby recently released her international bestselling book, *I See Your Genius*, which is available on Amazon.

Shelby's consulting and executive coaching expertise has spanned many industries and careers, including non-profit organizations, real estate agents, government agencies, and other small businesses. She has been asked to speak at training sessions for several large companies and is also central to advanced manager training sessions with her local university.

Shelby has been a professor and director of the debate program at Rocky Mountain College since 2006.

Please learn more about all of the amazing work Shelby does at shelbyjolong.com.

PIVOT Magazine

Founder and President
Jason Miller
jason@strategicadvisorboard.com

Editor-in-Chief
Chris O'Byrne
chris@jetlaunch.net

Design
JETLAUNCH.net

Advertising
Chris O'Byrne
chris@jetlaunch.net

Webmaster
Joel Phillips
joel@proshark.com

Editor
Laura West
laura@jetlaunch.net

Cover Design
Debbie O'Byrne

FROM THE DESK OF THE PRESIDENT

6 Steps to Improve Your Company's Culture and Allow It to Reach Its Full Potential

Jason Miller

Company culture is a crucial aspect of any business, impacting employee morale, customer satisfaction, and ultimately, the bottom line. However, if your company culture is not up to par, it can hold your business back and prevent it from reaching its full potential. In this article, we outline six steps you can take to improve your company culture and allow it to reach its full potential.

From defining your company values and communicating them to your employees to fostering a positive work environment and recognizing your team's hard work, these steps will help you create a strong and healthy company culture that can drive success.

What is culture, and why is it important?

Culture refers to the shared beliefs, values, customs, behaviors, and practices that

characterize a group or organization. It is a company's unique identity, shaping how employees interact with each other and customers.

Culture is important because it can have a significant impact on the success of a business. For example, a positive company culture can lead to increased employee morale and retention, higher customer satisfaction, and ultimately, greater success for the business. On the other hand, negative company culture can lead to low employee morale, high turnover, and poor customer satisfaction.

Company culture is key to reaching its full potential. A strong company culture is essential for a business to reach its full potential. It sets the tone for the way that employees interact with each other and with customers, and it can have a significant impact on the success of the business.

By focusing on building a positive company culture, businesses can create a supportive and inclusive environment that encourages collaboration and innovation. This, in turn, can lead to increased employee morale and retention, higher customer satisfaction, and ultimately, greater success for the business.

On the other hand, a negative company culture can hold a business back and prevent it from reaching its full potential. It can lead to low employee morale, high turnover, and poor customer satisfaction, all of which can hinder the growth and success of the business.

In conclusion, company culture is key to reaching the full potential of a business.

By focusing on building a positive and supportive culture, businesses can create an environment that encourages collaboration, innovation, and success.

As a business owner or manager, you know that company culture is crucial to the success of your business. It affects everything from employee morale and retention to customer satisfaction and the bottom line. If your company culture is not up to par, it can hold your business back and prevent it from reaching its full potential.

So, how do you go about improving your company culture and allowing it to reach its full potential? Here are six steps you can take.

1. Define your company culture

Defining your company culture is an important step in the process of improving your company culture and allowing it to reach its full potential. Your company culture is the unique identity of your business, and it shapes the way that employees interact with each other and with customers. By defining your company culture, you can establish the values and behaviors that are important to your business and ensure that they are reflected in all aspects of your company culture.

Here are some steps you can take to define your company culture:

Identify your core values: What are the values that are most important to your business? These values should be reflected in all aspects of your company culture.

Communicate your values: Make sure that all employees understand your company values and how they should be reflected in their work.

Hire for fit: When hiring new employees, make sure they align with your company values and will fit in with your company culture.

Establish company-wide policies and procedures: Establish policies and procedures that reflect your company values and support a positive company culture.

Lead by example: As a leader, it's important to model the values and behaviors you want to see in your company culture.

By defining your company culture, you can establish a clear set of values and behaviors that will shape the way that employees interact with each other and with customers. This, in turn, can help improve your company culture and allow it to reach its full potential.

2. Promote a positive work environment

Promoting a positive work environment is an important step in the process of improving your company culture and allowing it to reach its full potential. A positive work environment can have a significant impact on employee morale and productivity, and it can ultimately contribute to the success of your business.

Here are some steps you can take to promote a positive work environment:

Create a welcoming and inclusive atmosphere: Make sure that your workplace is welcoming and inclusive and that all employees feel valued and supported.

Foster a culture of respect: Create a culture of respect by promoting open and honest communication and by treating all employees with kindness and respect.

Encourage work-life balance: Encourage work-life balance by offering flexible work arrangements and promoting a healthy work-life balance for all employees.

Provide resources for employee well-being: Offer resources such as employee assistance programs and wellness programs to support the well-being of your employees.

Recognize and reward hard work: Recognize and reward the hard work and contributions of your employees. This can help motivate and engage employees and foster a positive work environment.

By promoting a positive work environment, you can create a supportive and inclusive atmosphere that encourages collaboration, innovation, and success. This, in turn, can help improve your company culture and allow it to reach its full potential.

3. Encourage creativity and innovation

Encouraging creativity and innovation is an important step in the process of improving your company culture and allowing it to reach its full potential. Creativity and innovation can help your business stay competitive and drive growth, and a culture that encourages these qualities can foster a sense of innovation and collaboration among employees.

Here are some steps you can take to encourage creativity and innovation in your company culture:

Foster a culture of continuous learning: Encourage employees to learn and grow professionally by providing opportunities for professional development and training.

Encourage employees to share their ideas: Encourage employees to share their ideas and suggestions for improvement. This can help foster a sense of ownership and encourage innovation.

Encourage risk-taking: Encourage employees to take risks and try new things. This can help foster a culture of innovation and drive growth.

Create a supportive and inclusive environment: Create a supportive and inclusive environment that encourages collaboration and innovation.

Recognize and reward creative ideas: Recognize and reward creative ideas and contributions. This can help motivate and engage employees and encourage creativity and innovation.

By encouraging creativity and innovation, you can create a culture that fosters collaboration and drives growth. This, in turn, can help improve your company culture and allow it to reach its full potential.

4. Celebrate team successes

Celebrating team successes is an important step in the process of improving your company culture and allowing it to reach its full potential. By recognizing the hard work and achievements of your employees, you can foster a sense of accomplishment and pride in the work that they do. This, in turn, can help motivate and engage employees and contribute to a positive company culture.

Here are some steps you can take to celebrate team successes:

Share team successes with the company: Share the achievements of your teams with the rest of the company. This can help foster a sense of pride and accomplishment among all employees.

Celebrate team successes publicly: Consider celebrating team successes publicly, such as through social media or in company-wide meetings. This can help build morale and encourage a sense of pride in the company.

Take the time to celebrate: Make sure to take the time to celebrate team successes and show your appreciation for the hard work and achievements of your employees.

By celebrating team successes, you can foster a positive company culture and motivate and engage your employees. This, in turn, can help improve your company culture and allow it to reach its full potential.

5. Recognize individual contributions

Recognizing individual contributions is an important step in the process of improving your company culture and allowing it to reach its full potential. By acknowledging the hard work and achievements of your employees, you can foster a sense of accomplishment and pride in the work that they do. This, in turn, can help motivate and engage employees and contribute to a positive company culture.

Here are some steps you can take to recognize individual contributions: Provide regular feedback: Provide regular feedback to your employees to let them know how they are doing and to recognize their contributions.

Recognize and reward individual achievements: Recognize and reward the achievements of your employees. This can be in the form of verbal recognition, written recognition, or rewards, such as gift cards or individual outings.

Share individual achievements with the company: Share the achievements of your employees with the rest of the company. This can help foster a sense of pride and accomplishment among all employees.

Recognize individual contributions publicly: Consider recognizing individual contributions publicly, such as through social media or in company-wide meetings. This can help build morale and encourage a sense of pride in the company.

By recognizing individual contributions, you can foster a positive company culture and motivate and engage your employees. This, in turn, can help improve your company culture and allow it to reach its full potential.

6. Support employee empowerment

Supporting employee empowerment is an important step in the process of improving your company culture and allowing it to reach its full potential. By empowering your employees, you can give them the autonomy and support they need to take ownership of their work and make decisions. This can help foster a sense of ownership and accountability among your employees and contribute to a positive company culture.

Here are some steps you can take to support employee empowerment:

Provide training and development opportunities: Provide your employees with training and development opportunities to help them grow and develop their skills.

Encourage decision-making: Encourage your employees to make decisions and take ownership of their work.

Provide support and resources: Provide your employees with the support and resources they need to succeed in their roles.

Foster open communication: Encourage open and honest communication between employees and management to help create a collaborative and supportive environment.

Delegate responsibility: Delegate responsibility and give your employees the autonomy they need to take ownership of their work.

By supporting employee empowerment, you can create a culture that encourages collaboration, innovation, and success. This, in turn, can help improve your company culture and allow it to reach its full potential.

The bottom line is that a good culture attracts great people and keeps them happy. So, it's not just about having an awesome company culture but also making sure you are adopting the best possible steps to create such a great environment.

As you can see in the list above, there are six steps you can follow right now to improve your company's culture and make it one of the best places to work later on. Stick to one or two of these steps, and your new and improved work culture will soon be on its way!

THE GENIUS ENTREPRENEUR

SHELBY JO LONG

Creating a brand that stands out in the digital marketplace is on every business owner's mind. Unfortunately, it becomes more challenging to connect with your ideal clients in this digital world. When you create a brand around your genius, you invite your audience to connect with you on an emotional level. This emotional connection helps your message resonate with the audience.

Your brand story helps connect your genius to a new audience on an emotional level. Using your genius, you will serve as a guide and a coach to your new clients in their transformation process. The relationship deepens with your clients, and you create a community surrounding your genius idea. Genius doesn't exist in a bubble, especially when you are generating transformation in your clients.

You enter a marketplace when you place a monetary value on your genius solution. Like small-business owners in the digital world, genius entrepreneurs have to think about attracting their ideal clients. In the flooded world of digital marketing, a clear story of your brand and the results of your transformation are how you stand out against your competition.

Your brand story explains who you are and your genius process. This narrative helps your new audience understand the solution and transformation from a firsthand account, besides establishing your credibility around the service you provide. Your potential clients want to see the transformation and understand the results of the process. When clients invest in a transformation, they want to know what to expect in the process and the results of their investment.

Customers invest in solutions to challenges in their business or their life. Your brand story helps make that journey a tangible process that connects with clients on an emotional and logical level.

Your Marketplace Competition

A clear understanding of the market landscape is necessary as you introduce your brand to a new audience. Knowing your competition within this audience helps you better communicate and create a connection with them. You can then situate your offer with the ideal client base that is the best match for your genius product.

First, think about the results of your transformative journey. When your unique process results in more time, freedom, clients, or money, clients will invest. Clearly identify the results that your clients can expect if they become involved with your genius journey. The journey was meaningful to you because it impacted your business or your lifestyle, but it becomes a journey that

your clients also want to take. That makes it genius. But other people are providing similar results within the same context; they are your competition.

So how do you identify your competition? Get into the market. Understanding who is in this new audience helps you understand where they spend time. Do they spend time in certain groups on social media outlets or on certain websites? And who is speaking to this audience in each digital space? Knowing your competition becomes central to how you clarify the process of your genius and how you talk about the results. The greater your awareness of the offers that are already out there, the better you can shape your genius uniquely. The more you know about your competition in that market, the better your competitive advantage when you market your genius product.

Know your target market and what problems they seek to solve. Enter the market with a new branded idea that will create change within that niche. Your brand and your brand story are crucial to making this connection.

Many small businesses don't consider their surroundings as they develop their business launch and marketing plans. I've seen many entrepreneurs—myself included—who developed their businesses in a vacuum.

We work hard to develop our ideas/products/services and design our business and administrative processes. We build our mailing list and create our messages, email templates, and customer message templates. We have these things set in place, but if we haven't considered the environment we're in or the competition that's out there, how do we differentiate from our competition? Your brand and your brand story separate your genius solution from your competitors. This is a critical lesson that entrepreneurs must learn to be successful.

You may have a great argument, but if you're not considering the client's concerns, your response to their argument, or what your competition is saying, then your message will fall flat. So, a dynamic understanding and engagement between you and your clients will help you develop messages that connect and resonate with each client.

That lesson has been embedded in my consciousness since my debate days. I may have a great argument, but if I'm not considering who the competition is and what they are saying, or considering my response to their argument, then my message will fall flat. It's this dynamic understanding and engagement in the moment. The same dynamics and real-time engagement in debate are also true for entrepreneurs of genius business solutions. Unless you understand the landscape of competition, your idea won't stand out in the noise of marketing.

This is why market analysis is so key. If you're opening a restaurant in an area that has multiple restaurants, then you must analyze your market to determine why people will choose your restaurant over somebody else's. The same is true in this digital economy, where we have to tell our stories to connect with potential clients on an emotional level so we can stand out from the competition.

Your brand story is the most powerful tool in marketing your business. Consumers buy brands they trust because they are emotionally connected to the stories. I help my clients think about their images, what they're promoting, the messages they're sending, and whether they are right for their audience.

Your genius is unique, but when you tell the story that is behind your genius, you create an influential and memorable brand that differentiates you from your competitors.

Genius Entrepreneurship

Clarity in the niche you serve, the problem you solve, and the impact of your solution is the magic of transforming your expertise into a successful business.

Identifying a clear niche audience keeps you in your lane. It also helps you deepen relationships with your clients and develop strong repeat business and a healthy referral flow for your service. Staying in your lane also helps you stay in your space of innovation and creativity, where you can test offers with your client community and create more solutions within your group. When you create this market match, you master the communication with your target market. When this trust is built, it allows you to continue to innovate and create to solve additional problems for your audience. This trust allows you to expand your genius business, deepen your impact in the target market, and emerge as an expert in this new community.

Think of an accountant who helps businesses with their bookkeeping, taxes, and financial planning. Good accountants make themselves indispensable to small businesses because they meet the multiple needs of entrepreneurs through various stages of business development and growth. Think of a chiropractor who not only fixes your immediate back pain but also has a physical fitness program and a nutrition program to provide their clients with the best solutions for their health. Or a marketing agency that can take care of your advertising development and marketing strategy and has the tools to implement the strategy. These types of companies have continued to develop and solve problems for their audiences to deepen their trust and connection with their clients.

They identify an audience, create solutions to problems with their tools and resources, and invest in long-term relationships with their clients. Here's another example: Think of a real estate agent who has helped you find your house and also walked you through the entire client journey of selling your current home, identifying your desired neighborhood and school district, and directing you toward financing and contractor resources. By doing so, they smoothed the journey and helped you avoid some challenges you may confront in buying and selling a house.

Your genius has the same opportunity. You solve problems and provide expert support and connections to resources to help manage the challenges they may confront in their business.

The magic of your genius is in how you adapt to your new audience and create a community surrounding your ideas.

Entrepreneurship is a journey. The economy goes up and down, consumer behaviors change, and it is challenging to maintain consistency in your production and services. You need to mentally prepare yourself for these challenges.

In addition, you must be prepared for a lack of engagement or even the rejection of your ideas in the marketplace. You must be ready to pivot your approach and respond to the needs of the audience. This is why the careful construction of your genius, a plan for execution, and the ability to adapt your communication style are critical for your genius journey.

Genius is Intuition

The true magic of creation emerges in your genius program when you allow yourself to follow your intuition. Pay attention to the processes you gravitate toward during your daily practices and the foundational skills that emerge in your workspace. You practice and develop these skills throughout different business contexts, and it often takes deep reflection or a third party to help you realize your potential.

An example from my own business experience, and my reflection on my skill, is in my messaging. My years as a college professor and debate participant and coach have helped me focus on the skill of developing concise and memorable messages. If you don't draw your audience's attention to the important takeaways from your speech or presentation, then your main points will not resonate with your audience. You become much more influential in your communication with clear, concise, and impactful messages that call attention to the value of your message to the audience.

Intuition also manifests in instant synergy in business partnerships. When you are confident in your skills, your offer, and your genius, then others will be drawn to you. Your message becomes clearer, and you step into the solution where you have an immense passion. Clients will be attracted to you because you are creating a community that surrounds the journey, and you are leading them through solutions. Your intuition creates synergy and the potential for business partnerships that extend your business reach.

Step into thought leadership and genius entrepreneurship.

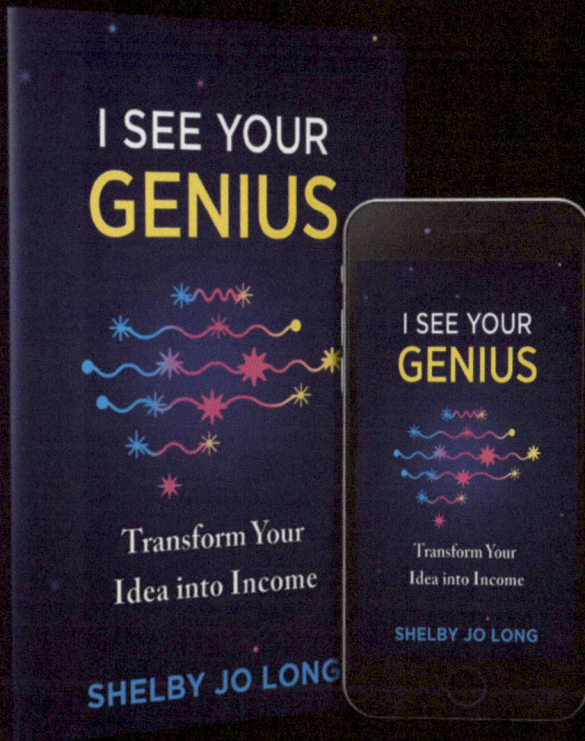

FROM LIGHTING TO SUBS

JR EDENS

I grew up in the lighting industry. My father was in it for 40 years before me, so I grew up in it. Seeing my dad in that business for as long as he was and all the hours he had to travel to build the business took away any passion I had to go that route.

When I went to college, my goal was to be a pilot for an airline, but after September 11, they changed the regulations and hour requirements. This made it tough for me since I had health issues that wouldn't allow me to take the military route and get my flight time hours up.

While in college, I was also a district manager for a large movie theater chain. But it was purchased by an investment company, and they were laying off those positions. So, I got my degree and went to my father and said, "Let's try this lighting thing and see how it goes."

Twenty-two years later, I had built a nice life, but the passion wasn't there. So last year, I looked at my wife and said, "If I don't take the leap and pursue this entrepreneurial passion that I have, I will never leap. I want to leave a legacy for our two young daughters and set them up for ownership opportunities when they get out of college that I didn't have."

I started a small lighting business with a colleague early in 2022. However, I also needed something that paid the bills. I wanted to do something that helped the community as well. So, I started down the path of franchise ownership and wound up with Firehouse Subs.

As the owner of multiple Firehouse Subs locations, we serve great food, have great customer service, and help the community through our Public Safety Foundation.

Our customers are looking for great food and a great environment at a great price. We provide subs cooked when you order, a variety of salads, great soups, and amazing chili. Firehouse Subs are considered the top-shelf subs at the best prices.

I was in the process of opening a sub shop from a competitive brand based out of the northeast and couldn't handle being lied to about different things through the process. I asked them who their biggest competitor was, and now, I own two locations and am building a third. I hope to have four by the middle of 2024.

During the first week in ownership, one of the locations' fire departments had put in a grant request for new hazmat gear since theirs' was many years old and wasn't working. I got it approved right away, and we got them $6,000 to buy all new hazmat equipment for the entire department.

Since I have been in the construction business for so long, I also started a business remodeling and flipping houses.

When you are looking for purpose and legacy, first, you need to know what that is for you and then follow the passion to get there.

My purpose is to help people, lead people, and learn how to be a better person daily. My legacy is how I leave this world for my two daughters and how they have opportunities for better lives.

2022 has been a year of growth and a year I took a leap of faith. 2022 was also a year of looking at P&Ls—not Profit and Loss

Statements, even though you need to understand those when being a business owner. But 2022 was a year of looking at a different P&L—Purpose and Legacy Statement.

If you want help exploring your passions and creating opportunities, call me, and we can make it work.

My business venture has been a leap of faith to follow a passion for leaving a legacy for my kids. Anyone interested in or dreaming of doing the same, reach out to me, and I can help you find your purpose and legacy.

You can find more information on my LinkedIn and Instagram.

GROW SMART WITH GROWTH STACK

KEVIN PETERSEN

Our ideal customer is a medium-sized business that is seeking a higher volume of online traffic and conversions. Our customer base is mostly made up of eight-figure ecommerce brands as well as digital marketing agencies and SEO consultants.

Acquiring high-quality and high-converting online traffic is painful for most businesses. It can be very expensive without producing a high return on investment. Our solutions help founders and CMOs to optimize their marketing spend as well as their sales funnels to attract and convert more customers.

We provide a variety of online tools, including SEO optimization, pay-per-click management, digital PR, and content marketing.

Most of the managers and executives at Growth Stack are founders as well, so we understand what it takes for a visionary to take a product to market and grow it. We aim to help businesses grow in a smart way so they can earn new customers more efficiently than their competitors.

I was a nerdy kid. I started investing in the stock market when I was nine years old and went on to launch several companies before I was thirty. I participated in an IPO with founder shares in my twenties, and that helped launch my consulting career. I have experience working on big data propensity modeling and product launches for hundreds of startups as well as dozens of Fortune 1000 companies. Growth Stack was my way of merging my experience as a founder, advisor, consultant, and investor.

The most exciting feedback I have heard from a customer is that they received positive ROI on the annual cost of our program just seven days after subscribing. This is the type of value we deliver.

The easiest way to start is to schedule a consultation with one of our advisors or customer success representatives. I also run a mastermind for SaaS founders and investors. Any founder or marketer can benefit from meeting with us.

Anyone interested in spreading the word can meet with our PR manager to explore blog posts, podcast appearances, and LinkedIn promotions.

There are no shortcuts to success, and this is true for online businesses as well as brick-and-mortar. Getting online traffic and valuable customers is a process that takes time, energy, and money, so be prepared for the long haul. Focus on delivering value to your customers, and with an acquisition formula that works for you, you will be rewarded over time.

THE WRITE STEPHANIE

Since 2018

COPYWRITER

TheWriteStephanie.com

PLAN YOUR OWN BUSINESS RETREAT

KARA JAMES

The online space is noisier than ever, and to get clients, you have to stand out.

It is incredibly rewarding to help others build their businesses, and new coaches who can help you do just that are popping up daily.

To be successful, you must be unique. I know this all too well, and I coach my clients to find their unique voices and stand out from the crowd.

There are so many layers to what I do it can sometimes feel like looking in a fun-house mirror. I coach the coaches by helping them build their successful coaching businesses. I keep a strong focus on creating irresistible programs.

In addition, I set myself apart from the rest by being one of the "power of 10" advisors with the popular Strategic Advisor Board. I help CEOs with their offers and sales pages in my role there. I also work on the personal side of their businesses—onboarding and working within their strategic partner community.

My greatest strengths are my energy, zest for life, and being very down to earth. My authenticity and energy attract my clients.

As a business coach, I always look for ways to help my clients succeed. I've already made a significant impact with my main program, The Client Accelerator Program, which has aided coaches in developing and refining their coaching programs. And as an owner and director of the Strategic Advisor Board, I've been able to share my expertise with an even wider audience.

I also have a retreat hosting certification from the Retreat Boss to teach my clients how to lead beautiful retreats to sell their irresistible programs. This summer, I'll be doing this at my retreat.

Helping my clients curate business and a life-changing experience will be something they will never forget.

Business retreats are a powerful tool for coaches and CEOs looking to take their businesses to the next level. Not only do they provide a peaceful and distraction-free environment for clients to focus on their growth and development, but they also offer a unique opportunity for coaches and CEOs to connect with their clients on a deeper level and create truly transformative experiences.

Not only will I provide these retreats to my clients, but I'll also be able to teach them how to lead their retreats, providing double the benefit.

But as an entrepreneur, planning a retreat can be a daunting task. How do you find the perfect location? How do you ensure your program appeals to your clients? How do you promote your retreat and make sure it sells out? And perhaps most importantly, how do you protect yourself from potential liabilities?

These are all valid concerns, but with the right guidance and support, you can confidently plan and lead successful retreats that benefit your clients and help you grow your business and increase your profits.

But leading business coaching retreats is about more than just making money. It's about sharing your passion and expertise with others and helping them make positive life changes. When you lead a retreat, you can connect with your clients and affect their lives. This is not only fulfilling for you, but it also creates customer satisfaction that leads to long-term loyalty.

The most critical aspect of leading a business coaching retreat is customer satisfaction. The clients walk away with an irresistible program and the knowledge of how to host a retreat to sell that program they're proud of. The clients leave feeling inspired, energized, and ready to take on the world, and they'll be more likely to recommend your retreats to others and return for future events.

It's essential to focus on creating a positive and transformative experience for your clients rather than just checking off boxes

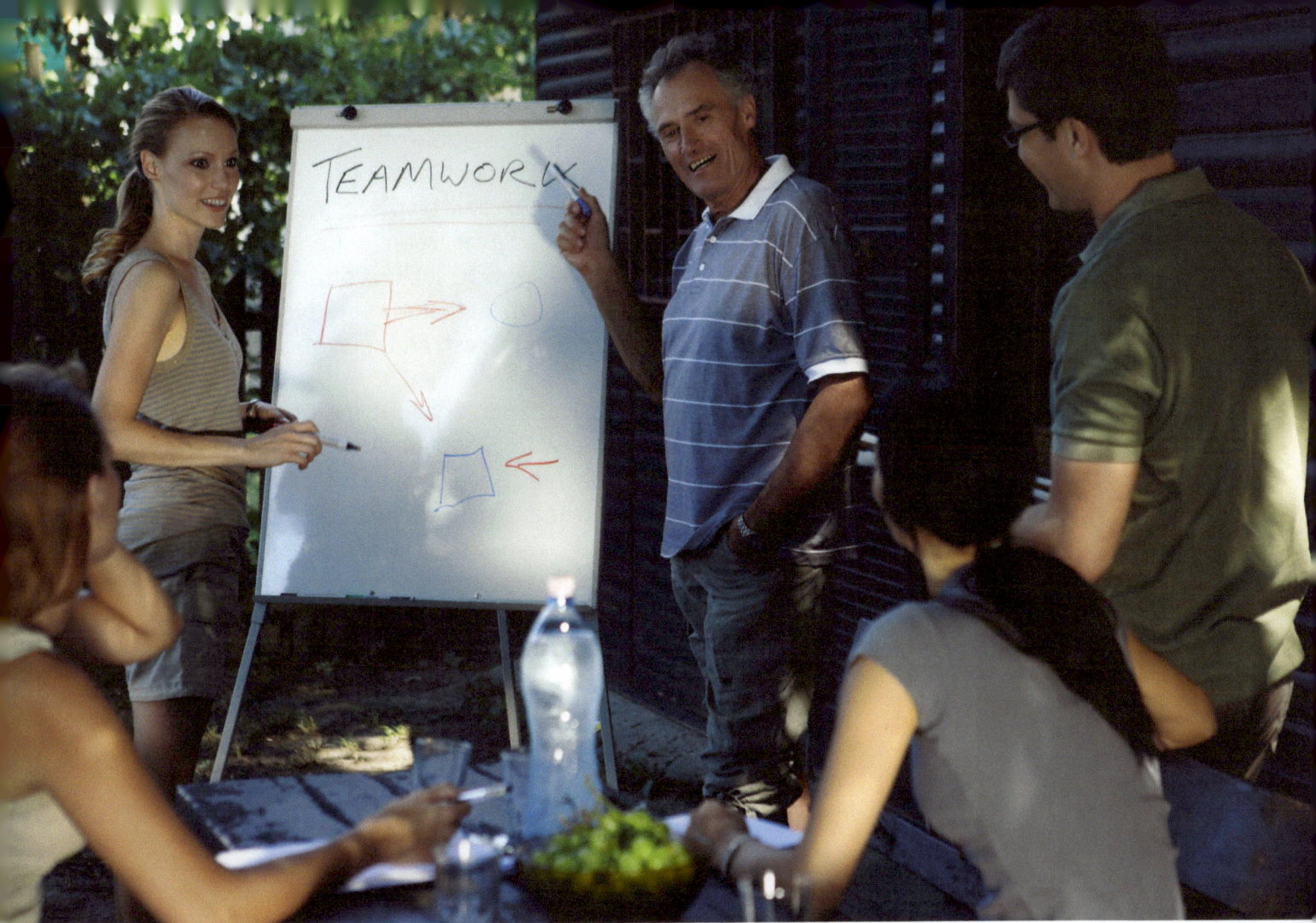

on a to-do list. By prioritizing customer satisfaction, you can build solid and lasting relationships with your clients and grow your business in a sustainable and meaningful way.

These reasons are why I am so passionate about teaching courses on how to lead retreats. I want to share my knowledge and experience with others, helping them plan and lead their successful retreats. With my guidance, coaches and CEOs can learn everything they need about marketing, budgeting, pricing, and post-retreat practices, giving them the tools and confidence to create transformative experiences. And with

the potential to triple their business profits by hosting two retreats per year, there's no reason not to get started.

My love for coaching and serving others stems from a near-death experience in February 2018. I am passionate about helping others stop living on the sidelines, jump in, take risks, and *live*. Follow your passion! The satisfaction of coaching others in my business and within the Strategic Advisor Board and helping them succeed, now in combination with a truly transformational experience while being in a breathtaking location, has brought my vision into reality, and I'm thrilled to help you do the same.

When people are given the right guidance and support, they can make positive changes and achieve their goals. And by sharing their knowledge and expertise and what helps them stand out, they can make a meaningful impact on the world.

A sneak peek at what a business retreat will include is my main program, The Client Accelerator Program. This is a comprehensive program that helps coaches and CEOs take their businesses to the next level. We condense that into four core pillars:

1. Irresistible offer creation
2. Compelling copy
3. Organic traffic strategies leading to an evergreen funnel
4. How to sell this offer at their own retreat (along with plenty of time for fun, rest, and relaxation)

To learn more about me and my advisory role with Strategic Advisor Board and my coaching programs, including upcoming retreats, visit www.pursueandthrive.com and www.strategicadvisorboard.com or email karajames@pursueandthrive.com.

THE ENERGY OF BUSINESS – A CRITICAL FACTOR OF FAILURE OR SUCCESS

MICHAEL SIPE

How often do we find ourselves powering through a difficult period or becoming victims of circumstances outside our control? No doubt, we have all experienced those moments in business. Yet, how we respond to those moments of trial drives the likely outcome from the energy we exude. Our energy determines our outcome both near term and long term. We all know that the people in an organization are far more influential than a company's product or service. Knowing and optimizing the energy they bring to the business is one of the most critical factors to business failure or success.

What Is Energy in Business

"Okay, big guy, so what do you mean by energy?"

There are quite a few definitions of energy out there. And even then, it varies a bit from people experienced enough with the term. So first, I lay out what type of energy I refer to in business. Then I talk about how it typically shows up in business. And last, I show you why it is so important to be energy aware as a leader and in an organization.

But first a story....

Janice had a chain of rotisserie chicken restaurants. She had spent eleven years building her business from scratch, starting with a simple takeout facility in a strip mall. Over time, she offered more foods, expanded into a new location with dine-in seating, and eventually franchised the restaurant into several restaurants around town. A lot of grit and hard work was the contributing factor to growth.

As was customary, the local county health inspector visited her facilities one day. Unfortunately, the inspector discovered what they considered a serious health violation and issued a citation to shut down all of Janice's restaurants. Talk about a setback. This was one of those business trial moments.

While working on a solution to get back open, she got some more disappointing news. She had one supplier of chickens, and the supplier notified her that the month's batches of chickens they had delivered were to be recalled for a flu outbreak. She kept these chickens in freezers and usually had about two months' supply on hand to cover all of her restaurants. Now her entire supply of product was wiped out. Her quick assessment was that she foresaw three months or even longer of being shut down. No cash flow and a threat of losing her eleven-year-old business.

For most people, this kind of scenario can be debilitating and even suck the life out of one to do anything. The classic response is typically a hopeless feeling. And that strong type of feeling is one of the three major contributors to energy: our personal energy.

Energy is the thoughts we think, the emotions we feel, and the corresponding actions or behaviors we take from those thoughts and emotions. For Janice, her thought was a very real concern for business failure. Her emotions were feeling helpless, despair, confusion, and sadness. Her resulting behavior was to retreat into her office and stare at the ceiling for hours.

Naturally, we all would respond in some similar fashion with that kind of energy. Those three parts of her inner world were driven by how she assessed her situation and defined her energy. Her energy is one of the lowest levels of energy, and it's catabolic energy because it depletes our body. It can consume us.

There are thousands of other thought, emotion, and behavior combinations. Generally speaking, though, they tend to fall into seven different energy levels. Two are catabolic, and five are the opposite or anabolic.

What's also important to know is that energy is not just individual; it's collective from other people. Organizations, businesses, and companies all have a collective energy, ever-changing and shifting. Yet, over time, successful companies have been

shown to have a higher resonating level of energy. In other words, it's not the quantity of energy a group of people has; it's the quality that is the key.

What Qualities of Energy are Typical in Business

Interestingly, most successful companies have and sustain anabolic energy. Those businesses that struggle more are those with more catabolic energy. The catabolic companies tend to react more like Janice had during her double-whammy setbacks, except these companies do it with less challenging situations. They see themselves as victims of external factors, or they are always in fight mode, trying to beat competitors or power through external factors they see as a threat. They see the marketplace as a perpetual struggle.

Anabolic companies tend to see opportunities, become more creative with products and services, exude greater teamwork and collaboration, and at a minimum, become acceptant of responsibility for their actions. In some companies, they get to the point where they expect good, and when it doesn't happen, they look for new opportunities to grow the business in a new direction. In fact, some companies become adept at seeing crisis as an opportunity.

After Janice spent some time in a catabolic energy state, she decided she needed some help. She spoke with her mentor and coach to help her get out of the funk. Through some exploratory sessions, she realized she could shift her product line and go into an area her customers wanted. She pivoted into plant-based foods and into an additional combination of products she could offer in her restaurants. She found an interim prepared food service company to supply her customers with new offerings. Her downtime of three months became only one month. It also bought her time to find multiple chicken suppliers to improve her supply chain and ultimately have a more diverse clientele at her restaurants.

Janice could have easily tossed in the towel early on with her huge setbacks. But her shift in energy to an anabolic curiosity allowed her to see opportunity in crisis. No doubt, that shift propelled her back into success and away from failure. Her story is applicable to all businesses. Ample evidence and research show that resilient companies are able to shift energy to an anabolic state more often than less productive companies.

Becoming aware of the thoughts, emotions, and actions we take as a leader of a business or collectively as a team helps us to sense our catabolic states of energy. It's up to us to decide how long we want to stay catabolic with setbacks. Success or failure depends on it!

AI AND MARKETING

JOEL PHILLIPS

Some of the hottest keywords in the business world right now have to do with AI (artificial intelligence), data sciences, NFT (non-fungible tokens), blockchain, DeFi (decentralized finance), and the always popular metaverse. There is a lot to unbundle, and many of these topics are intimidating, so rather than start picking them apart, we just go about our days in hopes we'll gain understanding through osmosis or that they will simply go away.

Neither of these strategies is bound to work, so the third alternative is to take some time to explore each silo on its own and then put together how they are interrelated and the impact they will have on us. In this article, we explore AI and marketing.

Before we get to specific applications, we should take a look at what AI really is. Then, when we understand it, we can understand how to apply it as a tool in marketing, customer management, relations, and a slew of other areas where using data and machine learning can create benefits and value for us and our company.

First, what is AI? In its truest form, AI is the application of data and machine learning to create an environment where computers can apply logic and data to deduce and reason in an effort to create an outcome or response. This means that machines would be able to "think for themselves."

In reality, the best we can currently do is to mimic intelligence based on robust datasets in an effort to, according to dictionary.com, "...perform operations and tasks analogous to learning and decision making in humans, as speech recognition or question answering."

The most common mistake people make is to confuse machines with having the ability to reason and make decisions based on the trillions of data points that we, as humans, take in over the course of our lives that help us build a decision tree based on experience. At most, computers, robots, and other processing equipment are only able to solve problems or develop answers based on data.

Where we experience things (events, education, transferred knowledge) and use that knowledge to make decisions, the learning process for machines is dependent on uploaded data. Therefore, the solutions these machines provide are only as good as the data AI entities are given. But why is this important?

There have been some significant advancements in AI, and it is difficult to remember sometimes that machines are just machines. Take, for instance, the fact that cars can drive themselves. We can provide dataset after dataset of road conditions, traffic conditions, human interface, and rules of the road. While cars and trucks are becoming increasingly better at navigating the process of operating a vehicle based on the

enormous amounts of data provided, what happens when the need for reasoning interrupts the process?

If, for example, the lines for a traffic lane disappear under new asphalt, what data does the processor use to formulate the next action? If the data isn't there, a human can interpolate data, whereas a machine has no data on which to base a decision. The datasets are consistently improving, as evidenced by where we are today versus even a few years ago. Data is getting better, storage capacity is increasing exponentially, and data transfer rates are getting faster with each new technology push, but the road is not all rosy ahead as AI and human interface continue to deepen.

Now that we better understand what AI is, let's explore how to use it to benefit us in the corporate world. First, there will be data aggregators and suppliers diametrically opposed to users and consumers of data. A very powerful example of this is Apple and what they are doing with data under the guise of privacy. Most people know that Apple, with the release of IOS 14.5, changed the rules with regard to third-party access to consumer data. What has always been available is now no longer available unless Apple users opt-in to sharing data.

Well, not quite. In one day, Facebook lost a staggering amount of market cap because they no longer had access to IOS data for advertising purposes. Now, marketing becomes more expensive and less effective. What Apple also didn't tell you is that they retained the right to use your data without permission. Oops! Did we leave that part out? It's okay. Nobody ever reads the Terms of Service, anyway.

To complete where we are going with this example, now that Apple is the only company with access to their user data, they just became a huge data supplier. Also, remember that nobody else has access to Apple data, and now every third-party will need to go through Apple. They currently own about 40% of the mobile market. As Apple data continues to grow and curate, the data will become far more valuable, and you, as a data consumer, will have to pay for it.

Given that the folks over at Google aren't dummies, they have already started following the Apple model and will shut down third-party access in the name of privacy by July 2023. Google owns the remaining 60% of the mobile market with Android. Google is already the biggest data supplier in the world. I'm not sure why they need to monopolize the rest, but they are doing so, and it is all in the name of privacy.

What does this have to do with artificial intelligence? Big tech is leading the way when it comes to putting up fences around data. This means that others will follow, but the premise of AI is that it needs volumes of data to function properly when automating processes to make our lives more efficient. How will the average marketer or business be able to function? The writing on the wall is that you need to begin collecting your own data and start doing it now. It no longer makes sense to offload it to big tech services. The rapidly changing data environment also means that you need to own your data where possible because data will become an extremely valuable commodity in the marketplace.

Data is not difficult to collect and connect when you have the right partner and process in place, but it is more important than ever to begin building your data store now. Marketing ROI is already diminished, but when retargeting disappears, it will get worse. It is crucial you are in front of the data curve.

We discussed several other silos at the beginning of this article, and it is important that we understand that all of these, including blockchain, NFTs, DeFis, data, and the metaverse, are interconnected. To survive the new economy, you need to understand and have a foothold in this brave and confusing new world. That conversation is for a different day.

PRIME COST AND THE IMPACT IT CAN HAVE ON YOUR BUSINESS

MIKE OWENS

With rising product costs and labor getting out of control, it's no wonder that independent operators are scratching their heads, trying to get a handle on their processes. One way to do that is to understand your prime cost, which consists of the combination of the manufacturing of products and total direct labor.

Most industries work off a model that manages these costs, but how often do they follow their own processes? In most cases, unfortunately, it's only on an annual or bi-annual basis. It's shameful, and they know it.

"I'm busy, I'm shorthanded, I don't have the right talent," and so on. These are all familiar excuses by independent operators who struggle to know their numbers. Those who are structured properly know these numbers weekly. Then, on the eighth day, they know what targeted issues need to be addressed immediately.

Why is prime cost important to an owner or operation?

For the seasoned operator, it's the one barometer that gives them an immediate indication of how well they are executing daily. For example, the prime cost will give an owner a metric of how well their contribution margin will help in determining what the price of goods should be.

In addition, the prime cost will give the owner a snapshot of expenses, efficiencies, and most importantly—profitability.

Prime cost is the one metric used for financial health when compared to sales and pricing a product correctly or even dropping an item that's margin deficient. Looking at your prime cost weekly tells you if your workforce is productive, where you need to pivot your model, or where to find crucial gaps in your business.

Let's look at an industry that really gets granular by using this metric to increase their basis points.

The restaurant industry is known for very lean margins and has little to no room for error. When a restaurant operator is looking at their prime cost weekly it helps make sound decisions immediately to whether or not the owner will to need to address the following concerns; purchasing, vendor contracts, menu engineering, recipe allocation, shrinkage, portion control, product yield, manufacturing processes, proper ordering, inventory turn, waste, theft, etc. It's all a delicate balance and this one metric will tell them the overall story of their operation. It's absolutely key.

While prime cost is a necessity, there is a level of caution that is taking place when it comes to buying ingredients or pivoting recipes, these practices can have a negative impact while trying to sustain customer loyalty. Saving pennies can cost an owner long-term customers, this is why recipe standardization and portion control plays an important role for consistency in product delivery. If these practices are not in place, you invite the risk of product over runs, unnecessary waste and even theft.

Food is only one factor of this metric. Labor is the other component which has an even equally important impact on the prime cost and trickier in terms of finding the right talent to manage efficiencies. Not being able to find or pay for top tier candidates, forces operators to push people into management roles without the proper training. This tends to backfire and leads to operational problems. To offset these decisions, operators lean towards raising prices, which impacts the losing of loyal customers as their standards are not being met.

These two factors (food and labor) or in the case of other industries direct material and direct labor makes up the formula for prime cost. It would be an understatement to say that minimizing the importance of having yourself as an operator or owner of not reviewing a short form P&L with your prime cost as the focus on what to discuss with your team on a weekly basis, this would be treason. Harsh? I don't think so because what's the alternative?

What is the formula for prime cost?

Well for restaurants, and not too much difference in other industries, but a prime cost of anything more than 70% is flirting with disaster, and below 60% you are a rockstar in the casual dinning space.

In the interest of time, let's keep this simple:

The first factor of the prime cost calculation would be direct material or product, which is the sum of all the physical ingredients that make up the end result or product. So, a restaurant that purchases ingredients to manufacture a dish to sell would be the materials for the end result of that dish. Any tool or other materials to produce that product, like a knife, storage container, labels, refrigeration, gloves, and so on would be an expense of overhead.

Just like a restaurant, a furniture manufacture, manufacturing a couch would count lumber, fabric and staples as direct materials. And the use of other materials used in production that don't end up in the final product, such as gloves, eye protection, and stapler for the furniture worker, would be considered indirect materials.

Here is the formula to get the direct material usage:

Beginning Inventory + Purchases - Ending Inventory = Direct Material Usage

The second factor of the prime cost calculation is direct labor.

Total direct labor includes the following:

- Hourly wages
- Salaried wages
- Sales commissions
- Benefits
- Bonuses
- Employer payroll taxes

The third factor of the prime cost formula is the sum of total direct labor and direct material or product costs.

Total Direct Labor + Direct Material = Prime Cost

For restaurants, as you can see, it's critical to have processes utilizing a metric like prime cost weekly, as it can have an immediate impact on one's business if actions are taken to minimize their risks.

Prime cost numbers may be different for other industries like construction or manufacturing, but equally as important to get the results that is needed to make sound decisions immediately.

No matter what your industry or metric of use is, understanding your numbers is critical and your prime cost should be your bible when time comes to review your operations output.

DOING GOOD IS
GOOD BUSINESS

SHARING THE CREDIT

Your business can give to charity without writing a check. Visit **www.SharingTheCredit.com** and start giving today.

PUBLISH YOUR OWN BUSINESS BOOK

CHRIS O'BYRNE

Publishing business books can be a challenging and rewarding endeavor, whether you are a seasoned author or a first-time writer. Business books cover a wide range of topics, including management, leadership, marketing, and finance, and they are an effective way to share your expertise and experience with a wider audience. In this article, we'll take a closer look at the process of publishing a business book, including the key steps involved and some tips to help you achieve success.

The first step in publishing a business book is to develop a clear idea for your book. This will typically involve brainstorming and outlining your ideas, researching the market, and determining the target audience for your book. It's also a good idea to read a variety of business books in your chosen area of expertise to get a sense of what is already available and to identify any gaps in the market that your book can fill.

Once you have a clear idea for your book, the next step is to write the manuscript. Writing a business book can be a time-consuming and challenging process, but it's important to set aside the time and effort to get it right. One way to make the process more manageable is to break the manuscript down into smaller, more manageable sections and work on one section at a time.

Once your manuscript is complete, it's time to begin the editing process. This will typically involve reviewing your manuscript for grammar, spelling, and punctuation errors, as well as for clarity and coherence. It's a good idea to have a professional editor review your manuscript, as they will be able to provide you with feedback on how to improve your book.

Once your manuscript is polished and ready for publishing, the next step is to choose the right publisher. Many authors prefer to publish their books through a traditional publishing house, while others choose to self-publish. Traditional publishing houses tend to have more resources available for editing, marketing, and distribution, but self-publishing can be a faster and more cost-effective option.

Marketing and promotion are also key components of publishing a business book. Many authors choose to promote their books through a variety of channels, such as social media, book signings, and speaking engagements.

Finally, it's also important to have a strong online presence. With the rise of digital publishing, having a strong online presence has become an increasingly important part of publishing a business book. This can include setting up a website, building a social media following, and leveraging online platforms to promote your book.

To conclude, publishing a business book can be a challenging and rewarding experience, but with the right approach and the right support, it is possible to achieve success. By developing a clear idea for your book, writing a quality manuscript, working with a professional editor, choosing the right publisher, and promoting your book effectively, you can achieve your goals and share your expertise with a wider audience.

6 WAYS TO GET A RAISE AT WORK (AND WHY IT'S IMPORTANT)

Are you feeling undervalued and underpaid at work? You're not alone. Many people struggle to get the recognition and compensation they deserve, especially in today's competitive job market. But with a little bit of effort and strategy, you can increase your chances of getting a raise and improve your financial situation. In this post, we'll explore six ways to get a raise at work and the importance of doing so. Whether you're just starting out in your career or have been working for years, these tips can help you take control of your financial future and get the recognition you deserve.

Why is getting a raise so important?

There are several reasons why getting a raise is important, both for your personal financial stability and for your professional development. Here are a few key reasons why it's worth pursuing a raise at work:

Increased financial stability: A raise can help you meet your financial goals and improve your overall financial stability. It can allow you to pay off debt, save for the future, or simply have more disposable income to enjoy the things you love.

Improved quality of life: A raise can also improve your quality of life by giving you more financial flexibility and freedom. It can allow you to afford things like a bigger apartment, a nicer car, or a family vacation.

Increased motivation and job satisfaction: Feeling underpaid and undervalued can be demoralizing and lead to decreased job satisfaction. By getting a raise, you can feel more motivated and fulfilled in your work, which can lead to better job performance and overall happiness.

Better job prospects: Having a higher salary can also open up new job prospects and opportunities for advancement within your current company or elsewhere. It can make you a more attractive candidate to potential employers and give you more leverage in negotiations.

Professional development: Finally, getting a raise can be a sign of your value and contributions to the company. It can be a way to recognize your hard work and dedication and can motivate you to continue learning and growing in your career.

Overall, getting a raise is important for many reasons, both financially and professionally. It can improve your stability, quality of life, job satisfaction, job prospects, and overall sense of accomplishment and value. Don't be afraid to advocate for yourself and ask for the recognition and compensation you deserve.

1. Demonstrate your skills

One of the most effective ways to get a raise at work is to demonstrate your value and contributions to the company. Here are a few ways you can do this:

Go above and beyond: Make an effort to exceed expectations and take on additional responsibilities whenever possible. Show your boss and colleagues that you are a reliable and hardworking employee who is willing to put in the extra effort to get things done.

Stay up to date: Keep your skills and knowledge current by staying up-to-date on industry trends and developments. Take

classes or seek out additional training opportunities to ensure that you are well-equipped to tackle new challenges and responsibilities.

Network: Build relationships with your colleagues and industry professionals and make an effort to understand the needs and challenges of your company. This will help you identify areas where you can add value and make a difference.

Communicate your accomplishments: Make sure your boss and colleagues are aware of your achievements and contributions to the company. Keep a record of your successes and use them to support your case for a raise.

Seek feedback: Ask for feedback from your boss and colleagues on your performance and areas for improvement. This will not only help you identify areas where you can grow, but it will also show that you are proactive and invested in your own development.

By demonstrating your skills and value to the company, you can increase your chances of getting a raise and improving your financial situation. Don't hesitate to take initiative and showcase your abilities.

2. Be a team player

In addition to demonstrating your skills and value to the company, it's also important to be a team player in order to increase your chances of getting a raise. Here are a few ways you can do this:

Collaborate with your colleagues: Work well with others and seek out opportunities to collaborate and share ideas. This will show that you are a valuable member of the team and are committed to working towards common goals.

Help out when needed: Don't be afraid to roll up your sleeves and lend a hand when others are in need. This could mean staying late to finish a project or offering to help out with a task that isn't in your job description.

Be a positive influence: Bring a positive attitude to the workplace and try to foster a sense of teamwork and collaboration. Avoid gossiping or complaining, and instead focus on finding solutions to problems and supporting your colleagues.

Be open to feedback: Seek out feedback from your colleagues and be open to constructive criticism. This will show that you are willing to learn and improve and will help you become a more valuable member of the team.

By being a team player, you can demonstrate your commitment to the company and your colleagues and increase your chances of getting a raise. Remember, it's not just about your individual contributions, it's about how you fit into the overall team and contribute to its success.

3. Advance in your career

Another way to increase your chances of getting a raise is to advance in your career and take on more responsibilities. Here are a few ways you can do this:

Seek out new challenges: Don't be afraid to step out of your comfort zone and take on

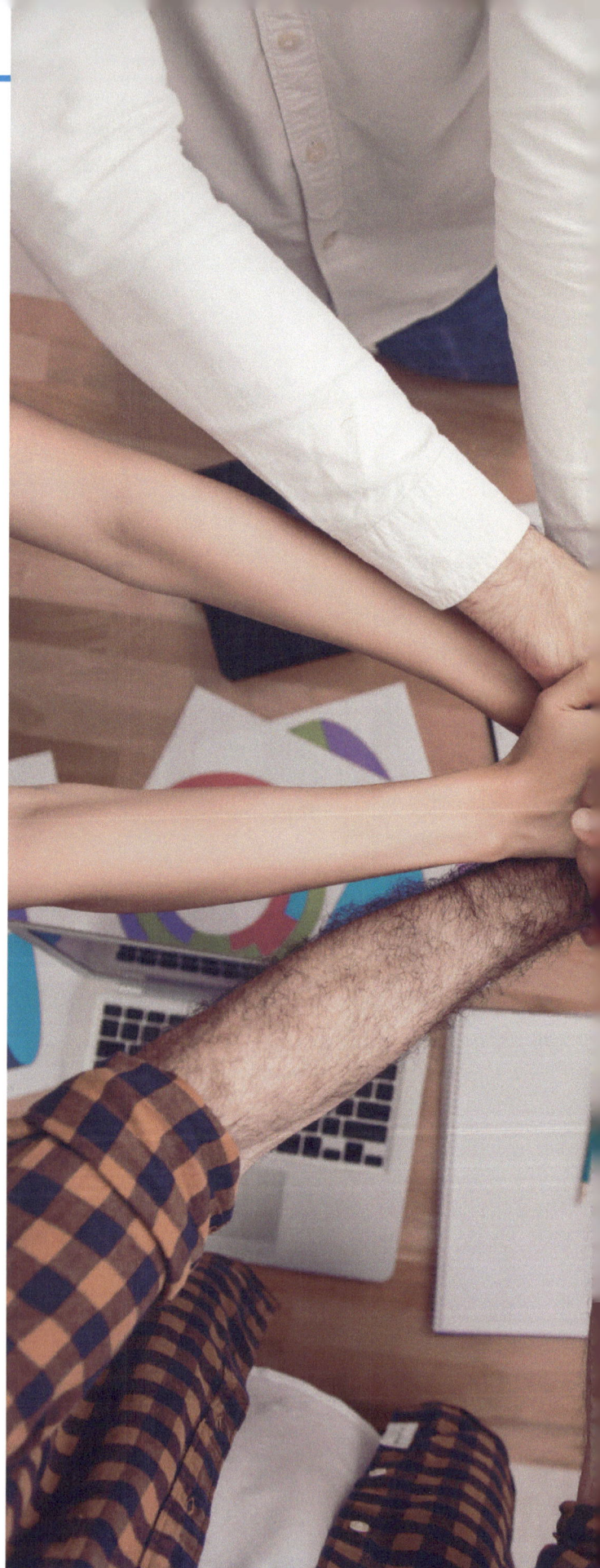

new challenges. This could mean volunteering for a special project, asking for additional responsibilities, or seeking out new learning opportunities.

Get additional training or education: Consider getting additional training or education to improve your skills and qualifications. This could be in the form of a degree program, certification, or professional development course.

Network and build relationships: Build relationships with industry professionals and seek out opportunities to learn from others. This will not only help you develop your skills and knowledge, but it will also increase your visibility and make you a more attractive candidate for promotions and raises.

Seek out opportunities for advancement: Keep an eye out for opportunities for advancement within your company and be proactive in seeking out new roles and responsibilities. This could include applying for internal promotions or seeking out new positions within the company.

By advancing in your career and taking on more responsibilities, you can demonstrate your value to the company and increase your chances of getting a raise. Don't be afraid to take initiative and pursue new opportunities – it could pay off in the long run.

4. Take on new responsibilities

One way to increase your chances of getting a raise is to take on new responsibilities and show your boss and colleagues that you are willing to go above and beyond. Here are a few ways you can do this:

Volunteer for additional tasks or projects: Don't be afraid to speak up and offer to take on additional tasks or projects, even if they aren't in your job description. This will show your boss and colleagues that you are reliable and willing to go the extra mile.

Seek out new challenges: Look for opportunities to challenge yourself and learn new things. This could mean taking on a leadership role, working on a special project, or learning a new skill.

Be proactive: Don't wait for opportunities to come to youm seek them out and be proactive in your career development. This could involve speaking with your boss about your goals and aspirations or identifying areas where you can add value to the company.

Take initiative: Don't be afraid to take initiative and come up with new ideas or solutions to problems. This will show your boss and colleagues that you are a valuable member of the team and are committed to driving results.

By taking on new responsibilities and showing your willingness to go above and beyond, you can demonstrate your value to the company and increase your chances of getting a raise. Don't be afraid to step up and take charge—it could pay off in the long run.

5. Don't be afraid to ask for a raise

Despite all your hard work and contributions to the company, you won't get a raise unless you ask for one. Many people are hesitant to ask for a raise, whether due to fear of rejection or a lack of confidence in their own worth. However, it's important to remember that your employer won't know you want a raise unless you ask for it.

So how do you go about asking for a raise? Here are a few tips to keep in mind:

Timing is key: Choose a time to ask for a raise when you are confident in your performance and the company is doing well. This could be after you have completed a major project, received positive feedback from your boss or colleagues, or when the company is experiencing growth.

Be prepared: Before you ask for a raise, make sure you have a solid case for why you deserve one. This could include a list of your accomplishments and contributions to the company, as well as any relevant skills or experiences you have gained.

Practice your pitch: Rehearse what you want to say ahead of time to ensure that you are confident and articulate in your request. Be specific about the amount you are asking for and explain why you believe you deserve it.

Be flexible: Be open to negotiation and be willing to compromise. Your employer may not be able to meet your exact request, but they may be able to offer other forms of compensation, such as additional vacation days or flexible work arrangements.

Remember, it's important to ask for a raise if you feel you deserve one. Don't be afraid to advocate for yourself and your worth.

6. Make your boss aware of your accomplishments

One way to increase your chances of getting a raise is to make your boss aware of your accomplishments and contributions to the company. Here are a few ways you can do this:

Keep a record of your achievements: Make a list of your accomplishments and contributions to the company, including any projects you have completed, goals you have met, or problems you have solved. This will give you concrete examples to reference when you ask for a raise.

Share your successes: Share your successes with your boss and colleagues, whether through email updates, status reports, or casual conversations. This will help them stay informed of your progress and contributions to the company.

Seek out feedback: Ask for feedback from your boss and colleagues on your performance and areas for improvement. This will not only help you identify areas where you can grow, but it will also show that you are proactive and invested in your own development.

Demonstrate your value: Make an effort to go above and beyond and take on additional responsibilities whenever possible. This will help you stand out and show your boss and colleagues that you are a valuable member of the team.

By making your boss aware of your accomplishments and contributions to the company, you can increase your chances of getting a raise. Don't be afraid to speak up and showcase your abilities – it could pay off in the long run.

Bottom Line

In conclusion, getting a raise is important for many reasons, both financially and professionally. It can improve your stability, quality of life, job satisfaction, job prospects, and overall sense of accomplishment and value.

There are several ways you can increase your chances of getting a raise, including demonstrating your skills and value to the company, being a team player, advancing in your career, taking on new responsibilities, and asking for a raise. Don't be afraid to advocate for yourself and seek out opportunities for growth and advancement – it could pay off in the long run. Remember, it's not just about the money—it's about feeling valued and recognized for your hard work and contributions.

ADVERTISERS

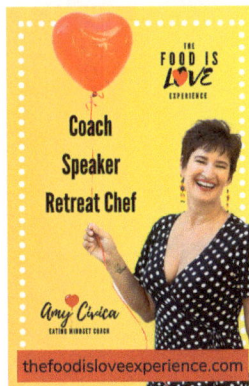

www.ingramcontent.com/pod-product-compliance
Lightning Source LLC
Chambersburg PA
CBHW041453210326
41599CB00004B/233